ECHOES FROM THE MOUNTAINS AND THE VALLEY

STORIES OF MY PERSONAL LIFE, SOCIETY, HEALTHCARE AND CHANGE IN KASHMIR AND LADAKH

DR FAZAL UL HAQ WANI

My Abu and Ami — For their unconditional love, sacrifices, and endless prayers that have shaped me into the person I am today. Their unwavering support has been my greatest strength.

My Brother, Mohasin — For always standing by my side, sharing my struggles and triumphs. Your presence in my life is a constant source of motivation.

My Mamu — For their invaluable guidance and wisdom, helping me navigate through life's complexities with clarity and purpose.

All My Family Members, including My Cousins — You have all been an integral part of my journey, filling my life with love, laughter, and cherished memories. Your encouragement has fueled my dreams and aspirations.

A special acknowledgment to The Kashmir Reader team, who provided me with a platform to express my thoughts and share my words with the world.

And lastly, to a special person in my life, who has always been there for me—through every high and low, offering unwavering support and encouragement.

May this book be a reflection of the love, support, and values you have instilled in me.

Contents

Contents

Foreword

Writing has always been more than just words on paper; it is a reflection of the struggles, emotions, and experiences that shape our lives. This book is a collection of my published articles—each one born from moments of deep reflection, personal loss, professional encounters, and social observations. These writings are not just stories; they are fragments of life that have left an imprint on my heart.

From the resilience of my late sister, Tehseen Didi, to the untold challenges of teachers in Kashmir, and the dignity of giving without seeking recognition—each article carries a message that I believe deserves to be shared. My journey as a medical officer in Ladakh has also allowed me to witness the silent yet profound struggles of healthcare professionals, which I have tried to capture in these pages.

But if there is one person who shaped the foundation of the person I am today—both as a doctor and as a writer—it is my beloved grandfather, Totha. His wisdom, strength, and unwavering belief in me became the guiding force of my life. He was not just my elder but my first teacher, my mentor, and the source of my inspiration. His values are etched into every part of my being, and

it is because of him that I stand where I do today. This book, in many ways, is also a tribute to him—to the lessons he imparted and the dreams he nurtured in me.

This book is divided into sections that reflect the themes of my writings—personal loss, societal issues, professional experiences, and philosophical reflections. Whether it is the heartfelt tribute to my sister, the ethical dilemmas surrounding charity, or a conversation with Waseem Sahab that left me pondering, every piece in this collection represents a moment of learning and contemplation.

I hope that these articles resonate with readers, spark meaningful conversations, and offer solace to those who find their own experiences reflected in these words. May this book serve as a reminder that stories, no matter how personal, have the power to connect us all.

Acknowledgements

If there is one person who shaped the very core of who I am today—both as a doctor and as a writer—it is my beloved grandfather, Totha. He has been my guiding light, my unwavering support, and the source of so much love and wisdom in my life.

I still remember the warmth of my childhood, those moments when he would carry me on his shoulders, making the world feel safe and full of endless possibilities. In his embrace, I learned what true strength and unconditional love meant. No matter how much time has passed, no matter how far I am from home, his presence in my life remains constant. Even now, as I navigate the challenges of my profession and personal journey, he calls me every day, ensuring that I never feel alone.

His belief In me has been my greatest motivation. He nurtured my curiosity, encouraged my dreams, and instilled in me the values that guide my every step. It is because of him that I have had the strength to pursue both medicine and writing, to stand firm in my convictions, and to always remember where I come from.

This book is not just a collection of my thoughts and experiences—it is a testament to the love and guidance that shaped me. It is, in many ways, a tribute to Totha, whose shoulders carried me as a child and whose words continue to carry me even today.

CHAPTER ONE

In Loving Memory: Honoring the Life of Tehseen Didi

A heartfelt tribute to a warrior who battled cancer with resilience, leaving behind a legacy of strength and love

In the quiet corners of our hearts, there are some sorrows too profound for words. It is with heavy hearts that we bid farewell to Tehseen Didi, a remarkable soul who graced our lives with love, strength, and resilience. Her journey with cancer may have come to an end, but her spirit will forever live on in the cherished memories we hold dear.

A courageous battle against cancer

In the chill of February 2023, a medical revelation unfolded, casting a shadow over our family. A routine endoscopy, initially anticipated to unveil routine matters, instead laid bare a harsh reality—an ulcer, a biopsy, and a diagnosis that would alter the course of her days. Carcinoma of the Gastroesophageal Junction, a formidable foe, announced its presence in the form of a Stage 3 diagnosis. In the face of this unwelcome intruder, Tehseen Didi emerged as a beacon of indomitable courage. Tehseen Didi's journey became a testament to the human spirit's capacity to endure, and to find strength where others might falter. Hersteadfastness during countless medical procedures and the harsh realities of cancer treatment painted a portrait of unwavering determination. In the echoing chambers of hospital corridors, she faced the complexities of her diagnosis with grace, turning each challenge into an opportunity to showcase her remarkable courage. Throughout the arduous battle that followed, Tehseen Didi's courage became a source of inspiration.

Amid the sterile halls of the SMHS hospital's oncology department, where hope and despair often danced a delicate tango, Tehseen didi embarked on a challenging journey of resilience. The battleground was marked by the rhythmic cycles of chemotherapy, each dose triggering a relentless onslaught of fever, nausea, and vomiting. Her body bore the weight of pain, an encompassing ache that left her unable to enjoy the simple pleasure of a meal, her stomach perpetually full. Throughout this tumultuous period, her steadfast husband stood by her side, a pillar of unwavering support.

Advocate Mudasir Baya, her younger brother, became a tireless guardian, navigating the labyrinth of emotions and medical intricacies to ensure his sister never faced the battle alone. With a nurturing spirit, he stood resolutely by her side, a steadfast guardian. His unwavering presence became a testament to the depth of his commitment, tirelessly looking after her with a level of care and dedication that mirrored a maternal embrace. In those moments, he became not just a brother but a nurturing force, providing solace and support with a love that knew no bounds.

Despite the hopeful moments post-chemotherapy, where glimpses of improvement sparked optimism, the cold reality manifested in CT reports that fell short of expectations. The medical journey took a darker turn as doctors prescribed radiotherapy, a phase marked by increasing fragility.

Yet, in the face of worsening circumstances, Tehseen Didi held onto her courage with an unyielding grip. Five times a day, she found solace in prayer, an anchor in the storm of uncertainty. Her unspoken trust in Allah transcended the realm of spoken words, a silent pact that held her heart steadfast. Blessed with two sons, she carried a serene faith, never burdening them with the weight of her impending departure.

Amid Tehseen Didi's arduous journey, her mother stood as an unwavering pillar of strength, a silent guardian concealing the tempest of emotions within. Though the world witnessed a facade of stoicism, inside, her mother navigated a landscape of grief, concealing the fractures of her heart with a resilience that echoed through her every action.

As cancer's relentless grip tightened, in the face of her daughter's battle, she chose not to break but to stand resilient, a sentinel concealing her emotional wounds while orchestrating a symphony of support for those around her.

Amidst the ebb and flow of hospital visits and home-bound struggles, a silent force emerged in the form of her brother's devoted wives. Standing resolute on one leg, they became the unsung heroines of Tehseen Didi's challenging odyssey. With a quiet determination that spoke volumes, Anjum Didi assumed the role of nurturer, providing sustenance for both body and soul. With tender care, she presented her with whatever morsel or sip she desired, striving to bring a semblance of comfort to the turbulence that surrounded her. Their silent gestures spoke volumes about the strength that family bonds can offer, even in the darkest hours.

Abida Didi's unwavering support and care for Tehseen Didi during her hospital stay and at home, preparing nourishing soups and fulfilling her every need, reflected the profound love and dedication of a sister.

Asad uncle's dedication in looking after little Azlan at home, ensuring he was cared for while Tehseen didi battled her illness, speaks volumes about the strength of family support during difficult times. His role, alongside the efforts of others, highlights the unity and love that binds a family together, especially during challenging moments.

Uncles and aunts, like guardian angels, descended upon the family home both in the brilliance of daylight and the quietude of night. Their visits were not mere obligations; they were threads of familial support, weaving together moments of solace and shared grief.

In the twilight of Tehseen Didi's life, as the whispers of inevitability grew louder, a singular wish emerged from the recesses of her heart. With a quiet determination, she entrusted her deepest concern to her brother, a plea that transcended the materialistic pursuits of the world. In those precious moments, she expressed a fervent desire for her two sons—a wish not for worldly riches or academic accolades but for a profound legacy of values.

Amidst the hushed conversations and shared glances, she conveyed to her brother a wish that would shape the future of her most cherished ones. It wasn't about accumulating wealth or chasing societal expectations; it was a plea for a different kind of wealth—for her sons to be nurtured with the richness of Islamic education, a spiritual inheritance that would transcend the boundaries of earthly possessions. In the simplicity of her wish, she painted a vision of a legacy rooted in faith, kindness, and moral compass. It was a call to prioritize the development of their souls over the accumulation of material wealth. Through the echoes of her words, she sought to ensure that her sons would grow not just academically adept but spiritually enriched, equipped with the teachings and values that would guide them through the intricacies of life.

The symphony of familial support for Tehseen Didi extended beyond immediate bounds, reaching out to include her other sisters and brothers. One sibling, studying abroad, paused life for two months, choosing to be a constant presence at her side, eschewing the allure of the outside world. Through the ebb and flow of days, this devoted brother remained steadfastly by her side. However, the somber notes of her final moments played out in a different setting. Despite the unwavering dedication, circumstances kept him in Turkey, physically distant during the poignant farewell. In the tapestry of care woven by her siblings, his absence during her passing became a poignant reminder of the unavoidable distances life imposes, even in moments of profound loss.

In the realms of medicine and familial ties, Tehseen Didi's words linger—a tender reflection of her care and affection. As a fellow healer, her gentle expression of concern, "I am giving you burdens; go study," encapsulates a deep understanding. In those moments, she didn't see me just as a doctor but as a sibling, urging me to pursue knowledge unburdened by the complexities of care giving. Her words, resonating with love, remain a cherished reminder of the unique bond We shared—a blend of professional dedication and familial tenderness. In missing her, her encouragement becomes a guiding light, symbolizing the enduring connection between a caring sister and a dedicated healer. The narrative took a poignant turn when, after months of battling, she felt the dizzying grip of bilateral pneumonia. The district hospital, recognizing the gravity of her condition, directed her back to the familiar walls of SMHS. Here, her oxygen-starved lungs became a poignant symbol of a body pushed to its limits. Despite the valiant efforts of medical professionals, the verdict was grim – survival for much longer seemed improbable. Returning home, the family created a makeshift haven with oxygen cylinders, a lifeline that sustained her for a fleeting week. As the days passed, her saturation plummeted, signalling the inevitable. In the poignant final moments at around 2:00 AM, Gowher Baya, her younger brother and her younger sister Asiya Di found solace in reciting the Qur'an for her relief. I, Abida Di, and Mudasir Baya surrounded her, tears falling from our eyes, a silent testimony to the deep emotions. As her oxygen saturation began to drop, we woke up her mother, brother Bilal Baya, and her husband, recognizing the urgency of the situation in those critical moments.

It was on a sombre November night, with the world cloaked in silence, that Tehseen Didi breathed her last. At 4:45 AM on the 27th of November 2023, her journey of strength, prayer, and unwavering belief reached its poignant conclusion.

May Allah grant the highest place in Jannah to her.

CHAPTER TWO

A Loss That Still Resonates: Remembering Tehseen Didi One Year Later

All the lessons she taught us and the sadness of her absence linger. We still carry in our hearts her words, her love, and her strength. Her death is still felt a year later, but so is her lasting legacy of faith, resilience and unwavering love.

Time finds it difficult to fill the emptiness left by the loss of a loved one. We lost our beloved sister, Tehseen Didi, to the relentless agony of stomach cancer one year ago on November 27 at 4:45 AM. That morning, she took her last breath in my lap, a moment etched into my soul that I can never forget. We carry that day's memory with us forever, a sad reminder of both her resilience during her illness and her absence.

In our family, Tehseen Didi was more than simply a sister—she was a beacon of hope. Although she led a simple and subtle life, her courage in her last months was remarkable. Despite facing an unrelenting illness, she maintained her strength, patience, and strong faith. Her spirit persisted despite her weakened body, giving us priceless lessons in patience and hope. Her final words,

"Take care of my children, not for material things, but to make them good humans," still have an impact on us today. Teach them to read the Quran and pray five times a day. These wise and kind comments from a mother now serve as a guide for our behaviour. My heart aches every time I see her two young boys, Umair and Rayaan. Their innocence serves as a reminder of the task she placed on us, which is to nurture their faith and character in addition to providing for their fundamental requirements.

As a doctor, I see many people who are struggling for their life. However, I am reminded of my sister's struggle each time I see someone who is really sick. Remembering her suffering and the silent courage with which she endured it, the connection is intensely close. I find it difficult to describe the state of the house in the last days of our sister's illness. Although we all knew what was going to happen next, everyone walked around with gloomy expressions and an unwavering sense of fear. The typical warmth and laughter in our house had given way to an unbearable quiet, broken only by whispers and the sound of muffled tears. The walls appeared to be mourning with us, and each and every corner of the home seemed to reverberate with our shared suffering. As we prepared for the inevitable, it seemed as if time itself had halted, imprisoning us in those painful minutes.

In addition to being an inspiration to me as a sibling, her story has taught me the value of faith in the face of hardship and the depth of empathy.

Despite living a modest life, Tehseen Didi left behind an incredible legacy of love and determination. She never gave up on her faith in Allah and taught us how to face hardship with dignity. For everyone who knew her, her bravery and faith served as a beacon, a reminder that even in the darkest times, there is light to lead the way. I want Allah to give her the greatest position in Jannah as we remember a year after her death. May He grant her children eternal peace and help them develop into virtuous, kind, and pious Muslims. Our goal is to honour her memory by raising her children the way she desired, which goes beyond simply fulfilling her wish.

All the lessons she taught us and the sadness of her absence linger. We still carry in our hearts her words, her love, and her strength. Her death is still felt a year later, but so is her lasting legacy of faith, resilience, and unwavering love. As we move forward, may we find comfort in carrying on the task she began, keeping her memories close. May her soul rest in eternal peace.

CHAPTER THREE

In Memory Of My Uncle

A tribute to my beloved uncle Abdul Ahad Wani who left an indelible mark on the hearts of our family and beyond

Some people stand out as sources of unshakable affection, pillars of strength, and guiding lights in the fabric of existence. My beloved uncle, the late Abdul Ahad Wani, was one of such people in our family. His love served as the glue that kept our family together, his wisdom served as a lighthouse to guide us through life's obstacles, and his presence was the cornerstone of our family. We honor a man whose memory will live on in our hearts forever, and whose effect was immense, as we reflect on his life.

The pillar of authority

Uncle was more than just a family member—he was a symbol of respect and authority. Everyone in the family sought his advice, from the youngest to the oldest, and his judgments were respected and trusted. His strong sense of justice, fairness, and compassion gave him authority instead of fear. He was an unwavering man of integrity and a man of principles. His advice helped us make sense of things when we were confused, and we never questioned his well-considered conclusions. He was the pillar of stability and guidance in our family.

A tapestry of togetherness

Uncle Ahad possessed an extraordinary capacity for skillfully connecting the strands of our family into a stunning picture of unity. He made it his goal to keep us in touch because he valued the strength of family togetherness. He made sure that everyone was there, whether it was a big celebration or a normal family meal. He would frequently remark, "We may not have many dishes, but we will eat together." This straightforward yet insightful worldview placed a higher value on community than on material wealth. We all have cherished recollections of the warmth, humour, and sense of community that pervaded his get-together. I recall numerous occasions where he went out of his way to bring the family together. He organized reunions, mediated conflicts, and always reminded us of the importance of staying connected. His efforts in maintaining family bonds were tireless, and his presence was a guarantee of harmony and joy. The gatherings he orchestrated were more than just events; they were expressions of love and unity, reinforcing the ties that bind us.

The echoes of departure

Our family was shocked and filled with deep sadness on the day my uncle passed away. His death came suddenly, like a blow out of the blue that left us stunned. Personally, it was like an earthquake to me when I heard the news, I was in Bangladesh, and it seemed like the ground was giving way under my feet. The anguish of his leaving was immense, and time hadn't completely healed the wound.

There is an unfillable gap left by his departure. But despite our loss, we take comfort from the experiences we had together and the teachings our uncle taught us. His spirit is still with us, a reassuring presence that keeps guiding and motivating us. His influence endures in our hearts, and the principles he taught us become the cornerstone of our existence.

Legacy beyond time

Uncle Ahad left behind a legacy that endures. Because of his efforts and influence, his family is now stronger and more cohesive than it was before. Our lives are still being shaped by his love, ideals, and teachings. His legacy serves as a tribute to the strength of purpose, devotion, and love—qualities that characterized his life. His life was an example of togetherness, love, and faith. His moral principles and the lessons he imparted to us continue to direct our lives. By upholding the values he held —integrity, compassion, unity, and faith—we pay tribute to his memory. His legacy is not just a part of our past, it is a living, breathing part of our present and future.

We honour the life of my beloved uncle Abdul Ahad Wani, who was full of spirituality, wisdom, and love. He was the cornerstone of our family, a man whose authority was respected, whose unceasing attempts to maintain our unity, and whose profound spirituality was deeply inspiring. Even though his passing was a great loss, his legacy lives on, influencing our way of life and helping us overcome obstacles. We pay tribute to Uncle by upholding the morals he taught us and by treasuring the memories we made together. His life was a blessing, and we will always have a special place in our hearts for his memories.

Uncle may no longer be with us in body, but his spirit remains, a guiding light that continues to illuminate our path, particularly for me.

CHAPTER FOUR

The Bittersweet Journey: Navigating Life Away from Home

Each step taken in a foreign land is a testament to the strength of the human spirit, an acknowledgement of the hurdles overcome in the pursuit of a better life

In the pursuit of personal and professional growth, many embark on a journey that requires leaving the familiar comforts of home. Whether driven by educational pursuits, career opportunities, or the quest for independence, this journey is often a poignant tale of sacrifice and resilience.

Leaving behind the embrace of parents, siblings, and the warmth of home, individuals venture into the unknown, driven by the necessity to carve out their path in the world. The decision is seldom easy; emotions run deep as hearts grapple with the desire to stay close to loved ones. Yet, the realities of life demand a departure, urging one to contribute to the grand tapestry of the world.

Studying abroad, for instance, becomes a testament to the pursuit of knowledge, often at the expense of the tender care and love of a mother. The aroma of home-cooked meals and the comforting touch of family are traded for lecture halls and academic challenges. The sacrifice becomes palpable as individuals strive to achieve academic milestones, driven by the hope of providing a better future for themselves and their families.

Working in a foreign land introduces its own set of challenges. The longing for the taste of home-cooked delicacies becomes a constant companion, a reminder of the miles that separate one from the familiar. Yet, the demands of the job, and the need to earn a livelihood, push individuals to adapt and embrace a new flavor of foods, often far from the flavours they hold.

The emotional toll of this journey is undeniable. Moments of exhaustion and homesickness collide with the necessity to press on, to fulfill responsibilities and aspirations. The struggle to balance personal well-being with the demands of a foreign environment is a silent battle fought by many, unseen by those quick to judge from a distance.

Amidst this complex tapestry of challenges and triumphs, the sacrifices made are often overshadowed by external perceptions. Critics may hastily assume that the journey is solely driven by financial means or the pursuit of a degree. The depth of personal sacrifice, the emotional toll of living away from home, is frequently overlooked.

In reality, those who embark on this journey face moments of hunger, emotional exhaustion, and the constant pressure to succeed. Yet, they persevere, driven by a resilient spirit that transcends borders and distances. The decision to leave home is not just a physical relocation; it is a profound choice to navigate a world that often demands more than it gives.

In celebrating the stories of those living away from home, it's crucial to recognize the courage and sacrifice woven into their narratives. Each step taken in a foreign land is a testament to the strength of the human spirit, an acknowledgement of the hurdles overcome in the pursuit of a better life.

CHAPTER FIVE

Insights from an exemplary civil servant: A conversation with Mr Waseem Ramzan

In the tranquil valley of Nubra, nestled amidst the majestic Himalayas, lies the abode of Mr Waseem Ramzan, a distinguished KAS officer from Ganderbal Kashmir currently serving as an SDM. Recently, I had the privilege of engaging in a conversation with this humble and down-to-earth bureaucrat, whose insights left an indelible mark on my conscience.

From the onset, it was evident that Waseem Sahab embodies humility and warmth. Despite his esteemed position, he emphasized the importance of eschewing any sense of superiority. "I am an officer in my office," he remarked, "but I never forget that my subordinates are not my servants; they are my colleagues." His emphasis on equality and camaraderie reminded me that titles shouldn't define how we treat others.

During our dialogue, Mr. Waseem Sahab shared a poignant reflection that transcended the confines of bureaucratic corridors. "Having all the comforts provided by the government, from transportation to accommodation, I often ponder: Do I truly possess the contentment of the heart? Do I lead a life imbued with tranquility?" These introspective questions underscored his quest for a 'sakoon wali zindagi' – a life suffused with inner peace and fulfillment.

In a society often fixated on material wealth and status, Waseem Sahab's humility serves as a poignant reminder of the essence of true satisfaction. He evoked the image of an ordinary employee with a modest salary, yet adorned with the tranquillity of the soul, juxtaposing it against his own circumstances. "Is the orderly employee with a meagre salary but inner peace not richer than me?" he mused, challenging conventional notions of success and fulfillment.

In a world marked by ambition and relentless pursuit of advancement, the wisdom imparted by Waseem Sahab serves as a beacon of light, guiding us towards a more profound understanding of success and contentment.

His humility, empathy, and unwavering commitment to serving not as a superior, but as an equal among colleagues, embody the essence of exemplary leadership.

In addition to his professional competence, Waseem Sahab's personal qualities have left a lasting impression on those he interacts with. Despite only a few meetings, he exuded warmth and treated me as a younger brother. His genuine concern for others is unparalleled; I have yet to encounter such kindness elsewhere. A defining moment was when I faced a transfer to another district. Waseem Sahab not only accompanied me but ensured my comfort and stability in the new environment. His reassuring smile spoke volumes, affirming his status as a true gentleman and remarkable individual.

As I said goodbye to Waseem Sahab, I couldn't help but feel grateful for our conversation. In just a short time, he had shown me the power of humility and the importance of finding contentment in life's simple pleasures. His gentle demeanour and profound insights left me inspired, reminding me that true greatness lies not in what we have, but in who we are and how we treat others.

CHAPTER SIX

To All My Colleagues, This One Is For You

As I sit down to reflect on our journey, I am filled with a mix of emotions – nostalgia, gratitude, and pride. Do you remember the day we embarked on our adventure to Bangladesh, leaving behind the comfort and familiarity of our homes to pursue our MBBS at Shahabuddin Medical College in Gulshan, Dhaka? We were young, ambitious, and determined, with a shared dream of becoming skilled doctors.

To put it simply, the first few days were stressful. The culture shock was real! The crowded streets, unfamiliar food, and humid weather were completely distinct from our experiences to date. I remember being scared and overwhelmed when I stepped out of the airport and seeing so many new people. The first few days were difficult, and I frequently asked myself why I had taken this risk. My constant companion was homesickness, and I longed for my family and loved ones. However, we continued and eventually started to adapt. Our hostel rooms became safe havens where we built long-lasting relationships. We encouraged one another during difficult moments and celebrated each other's victories. We helped each other go through the highs and lows together.

Our college days were a whirlwind of exams, study sessions, and clinical rotations. We worked tirelessly, fueled by our determination to succeed. We faced setbacks and failures but never lost sight of our goal. We made mistakes, learned from them, and grew stronger with each passing day.

I still remember the time I contracted dengue fever, and it was a harrowing experience. I was bedridden for days, and my condition was critical. But with the support of my friends and the medical care I received, I miraculously recovered. It was a close call, and I realized how fragile life can be.

We celebrated many Eids away from home, trying to recreate the festive atmosphere in our hostel rooms. Some days we fell sick but kept it hidden from our parents back home to avoid worrying them. Some of us lost dear ones back home, and it was a struggle to cope with the grief while being so far away. I lost my uncle in my third year of college, and I was devastated when I received the news. It was a terrible feeling, to be so far away from my family during such a difficult time. But we managed to support each other, and our friends became our family in Bangladesh.

It seemed like we had only arrived yesterday, yet time went by so quickly that five or six years had gone by before we realized it and it was time to return home. We cleared our MCI (FMGE) exams and began our careers, taking with us the knowledge, skills, and memories that would shape our future.

Today, as we stand at different crossroads in our lives, I want to remind you that our journey was not without challenges. We faced doubts, fears, and uncertainties, but we overcame them together. Some of us have secured jobs, others are pursuing junior residency or postgraduate studies, while some may still be struggling to find their footing.

To those who feel discouraged, I want to remind you of our college days, where we overcame countless challenges. Remember, everything has its time. Don't panic; you will do better. Just wait a little longer. Keep pushing forward, and success will follow. We did it before, and we can do it again.

As we move forward in our lives, let us not forget the bonds we formed, the memories we created, and the struggles we overcame. We are more than just colleagues; we are a family, united by our shared experiences and our passion for healing.

Best regards to all my colleagues

CHAPTER SEVEN

The Invisible Faces of Poverty: A Lesson In Kindness And Empathy

A Story of a Young Girl's Struggle and the Responsibility to Make a Difference

Some days ago, while on duty at our office hospital, I encountered a humble family who left a lasting impression on me. They were passing through our region on their way to Leh when their young child fell ill, likely due to the high altitude. I promptly attended to the child's needs, and as the treatment progressed, I found myself engaged in a heartfelt conversation with the father.

Our talk began with the usual topics—discussing the unique landscapes of Ladakh, the challenges and beauty of high-altitude travel, and the diverse culture of the region. However, our conversation soon took a deeper turn when the father shared an experience from their visit to Sonmarg the day before.

He recounted a seemingly simple yet profoundly touching incident involving his two young sons. Like many children, they had a particular fondness for Parle-G biscuits, and while they were dipping their biscuits in chai, a little girl from the area stood nearby, quietly observing them. She was clearly from an impoverished background, her clothes worn and her expression a mix of curiosity and longing. Noticing this, the father's elder son did something that, while ordinary to him, was extraordinary in its kindness—he offered her the entire packet of biscuits.

What happened next surprised the father. The girl, instead of eating the biscuits herself, took them to a nearby shopkeeper and exchanged them for a simple loaf of bread. This exchange spoke volumes. It revealed a harsh reality—the girl, driven by hunger and necessity, chose the more filling and practical option of bread over the treat of biscuits.

This incident struck a deep chord with the father, leading him to reflect on the broader implications of what he had witnessed. Here was a young girl, in the heart of one of the most picturesque places in the country, who was so deprived that she couldn't even afford the luxury of enjoying a small packet of biscuits. Instead, her reality was defined by basic survival, where a loaf of bread represented sustenance that could perhaps feed her for the day.As the father shared this story, I couldn't help but think about the stark contrast between his family and the little girl. His children, like many others in more fortunate circumstances, had the luxury of choice, of enjoying small pleasures without a second thought. Meanwhile, this young girl's life was a daily struggle to meet her most basic needs.

The father's reflection didn't end there. He began to ponder the broader failures of society—the growing chasm between the rich and the poor, and how the pursuit of wealth and luxury by a few often overshadows the dire needs of many. In a world where some are focused on building grand structures, luxurious malls, and acquiring material wealth, there are countless others who struggle to secure even the most basic necessities like food, shelter, and clothing.

This conversation left me with a profound sense of responsibility, not just as a healthcare provider but as a member of society. It's easy to get caught up in our own lives, to focus on our own ambitions and desires, but it's crucial that we don't lose sight of those who are less fortunate. The story of the little girl in Sonmarg is a stark reminder of the realities that many people face daily.This is why I felt compelled to share this story with you. It's a call to action, a reminder that we must always be mindful of the needs of others. If you are fortunate enough to have a stable home, regular meals, and financial security, you are already among the lucky ones. But with that privilege comes a responsibility—a duty to look around you, to see the invisible faces of poverty, and to extend a helping hand where it's needed.

Compassion and empathy should not be optional; they should be the guiding principles in how we live our lives. It's not enough to simply feel sorry for those who are struggling. We must take active steps to make a difference, whether it's through charitable giving, volunteering, or simply being more conscious of our consumption and how it affects others.

In conclusion, let us not measure our success by the size of our homes or the balance in our bank accounts, but by the impact we have on the lives of others. Let us strive to bridge the gap between privilege and poverty, to ensure that our success is not just personal but communal. By doing so, we can help create a world where no child has to choose between a loaf of bread and a packet of biscuits, where everyone has the opportunity to live with dignity and hope.

CHAPTER EIGHT

A Dream Fulfilled: My Journey To The Holy Cities Of Makkah And Madina

I had been dreaming for the last few years to go for Umrah with my family. I had always dreamed of traveling to the sacred cities of Makkah and Madina, but life, with its never-ending obligations and responsibilities, kept putting off my plans. The desire to see the House of Allah and the Prophet Muhammad's (SAW) final resting place, however, never diminished.

It was in November 2024, during the last week, that a sudden inspiration struck me. A voice within urged me to stop postponing and take this spiritual step. A special person finally convinced me to act. "Don't overthink," they said. "Book it now, or it will remain a distant dream." After consulting my parents, it was decided that my brother and I would go together.

I contacted a travel agent, and by Allah's grace, we got a departure slot for December 11. What followed was a journey packed with emotion, spiritual enlightenment, and amazing events.

The journey begins

The day finally came, and we set out on the morning of December 11th. After a short stop in Delhi, we changed into our Ihram and started to feel the spiritual weight of our mission. The flight from Delhi to Jeddah took six hours, and halfway through, at around 1:30 AM, a travel agency guide woke everyone up to perform the Niyyah (intention) for Umrah. The recitation of "AllahummaLabbaik, Labbaik" filled the cabin with feelings I had never experienced before.

We took a bus to Makkah after arriving in Jeddah around 2:00 AM. The air itself appeared to change as we got closer to this sacred city, filled with a sense of divine presence. We arrived at our hotel at about 3:00 AM in the morning. Even though I was physically exhausted, my heart was pounding, longing to see the Kaaba for the first time.

The First Glimpse of the Kaaba

After the Fajr prayer, we finally made our way to Masjid al-Haram. At around 7:30 AM, I saw the Kaaba for the first time. Words fail to capture the emotions of that moment. My heart was overwhelmed with gratitude, awe, and a deep sense of peace. Tears flowed freely as I stood before the House of Allah. Alongside my brother, I performed the Tawaf and completed the rituals of Safa, Marwa, and Halq.

The Moment of Halq (Shaving the Head)

When it was time for Halq (shaving the head), I experienced a profound moment of submission to Allah's will. In my daily life, I had never shaved my head. I didn't even cut my hair short it was something I had never imagined doing. But there, standing in the sacred land, I didn't think for a single moment about whether I would do it or not. The thought of bowing down to Allah's command and completing this Sunnah overwhelmed every other consideration. This act of shaving my head was a symbolic gesture of humility and surrender. It was a reminder that, in front of Allah, we let go of our egos, our preferences, and our attachments. We submit entirely to His will, trusting in His wisdom and mercy.

Seeing Makkah's Sacred Sites

We spent our days in Makkah touring important Islamic locations, such as JabalThawr, which provided refuge to Prophet Muhammad (SAW) during the Hijrah, and Jabal al-Noor, where Prophet Muhammad (SAW) got the first revelation. In addition to being physically exhausting, climbing these hills taught us a lot about the sacrifices made by our beloved Prophet (SAW) and his companions in order to propagate Islam.

The Holy City of Madina

We took a bus to Madina after spending 12 days at Makkah. There was a lot of excitement and anticipation during the trip. I felt a great sense of humility and shame, that how could I face Roza-e-Akdasbut I also yearned to arrive in the wonderful city where our Prophet Muhammad (SAW) is buried. How could the holy Roza-e-Akdas see me, a sinner? Though I begged for Allah's mercy and hoped that my visit would be a means of spiritual refreshment, the weight of my shortcomings weighed heavy on my heart. But I had an unimaginable calm as soon as we arrived in this beautiful city. There seemed to be serenity in the air itself. It was quite moving to visit Masjid al-Nabawi and stand in front of the Roza-e-Rasool (SAW).The first mosque In Islam, Masjid Quba, Masjid Qiblatain, where the Qibla was miraculously moved from Masjid al-Aqsa to the Kaaba, and JabalUhud, the scene of the well-known battle where many of the Prophet's

(SAW) companions were killed, were among the places I had the honour of seeing in Madina.

The Experience of Riyazul Jannah

One of the most important events in Madina was our appointment to enter Rawdah (Riyazul Jannah), which is defined as a section of Jannah where a believer's Jahanam becomes haram if they pray two rakats. Only once a year is this appointment given, making it a unique privilege. Unfortunately, two of the twenty men in our group were unable to join us since one of them became unwell and the other had urgent work to do. An hour ahead of our scheduled arrival time of 3:30 PM, at 2:30 PM, we reached Masjid al-Nabawi. Two random men came up to our guide while we were waiting and inquired about any open slot. Our guide let them join since we had two slots available.These two men were sobbing as we walked inside Riyazul Jannah, thanking us and telling us that they had been trying for a week to get an appointment but had failed. Their statement, "This was Allah's will," struck a profound touch. Through you, he summoned us. It served as a poignant reminder that only Allah's will can provide access to such holy places.

An Important Reminder: Avoid Excessive Shopping

Prioritizing ibadat over worldly diversions was one of the most important lessons I took away from my journey. We spent all of our time in Makkah praying and meditating instead of shopping. This relieved us of the burden of worldly worries and enabled us to totally immerse ourselves in the spiritual atmosphere. But we made the decision to go shopping in Madina, and it clearly affected our ibadat. Shopping took up time that may have been used for prayer, which was later regretted. I advise all pilgrims to minimize worldly distractions and concentrate on their main goal, ibadat. The opportunity to establish a close relationship with Allah in these holy sites is priceless, but shopping can wait.

An Astonishing Crowd, Yet Perfectly Managed

The huge number of individuals on this journey was among its most astounding features. There are literally lakhs of people in Madina and Makkah at any given time. The Saudi administration manages things so effectively in spite of this massive crowd. Despite the large number of visitors, I was amazed at how clean Masjid al-Haram and the surrounding area are. Thousands of people use bathrooms every day, and they are kept in perfect condition. Masjid al-Haram's grounds are so spotless that anyone can sit there without thinking twice. The crowd control, general organization, and cleanliness are all just amazing. I finally understood why Allah selected this holy location for the Kaaba.

Choosing the right travel agency

Selecting a reliable travel agency is one of the most crucial parts of this journey. During Umrah, a number of difficulties may occur, such as problems with accommodation, transport, to and from Masjid al-Haram and Masjid al-Nabawi, and meal plans. I firmly believe that travel agents should be open and truthful with their customers. This is a sacred journey, and it is crucial not to deceive people. Alhamdulillah, I was fortunate to have chosen a reliable travel agency, and I am deeply grateful to them for making this journey smooth and memorable.

Conclusion

The journey was a spiritual awakening as much as a physical one. It brought to mind the great benefits of faith and the sacrifices made by our Prophet (SAW). Alhamdulillah, I will always be thankful of this transformative event. I encourage everyone who aspires to see the holy cities to take action now and make their dream a reality. May Allah approve our efforts and allow all Muslims to travel to Madina and Makkah. Ameen.

The Pressure to Do More: A Silent Burden

In a society that measures worth by constant achievement, it's essential to reassess our value systems and find fulfillment in our current roles, prioritize mental well-being over the relentless chase for more.

We frequently find ourselves in a dilemma in today's world: even if we have everything, we nevertheless long for more. People may be wealthy, successful, and stable, but they still struggle to find peace of mind. This phenomenon is common in a number of sectors, including business, education, and other areas of life.

A never-ending race

There is an endless desire for more as a result of society's fast evolution. The system or social norms force people to reach more goals even when they already have plenty. Both mental and emotional health may suffer as a result of needless stress brought on by this pressure. Professionals in a variety of fields react differently to this stress. Even after reaching financial stability, a business owner may still feel pressured to grow out of concern that they may fall behind competitors. Students in education are frequently under tremendous pressure to obtain higher degrees not because they are interested in doing so, but rather to satisfy social expectations. People may feel compelled to always improve upon their prior work or adhere to commercial standards, even in creative industries like music and painting where enthusiasm should ideally be the driving force behind success. These demands are not unique to any one field, rather, they are a reflection of society's broader fixation with "more."

Personal Experience in Medicine

I have personal observations of this in my own life. After completing my MBBS, I currently work as a medical officer and make a salary that I consider more than adequate. However, neither my family nor the system are happy. Pursuing a postgraduate degree (PG) is implicitly expected, as though an MBBS is insufficient on its own. Sometimes, this push from society to keep moving up the qualifications ladder has made me doubt the choices I've made. Why did I initially decide to pursue an MBBS? Several professionals in a variety of disciplines are impacted by this pressure, so it's not just me.

The Dangers of Unrelenting Pressure

To be clear, I have nothing against the idea of getting a PG degree. My argument is this: is it insufficient for someone to stop at MBBS and give it their all in that capacity? I have witnessed MBBS interns consider their internships as mere formality because they are concentrating on their PG studies rather than wanting to obtain experience. The worth of the work they are performing now is diminished by this. According to my observations in the medical community, more than 70% of my coworkers feel psychological stress of some kind. This is frequently fueled by the unrelenting desire to obtain additional credentials, whether through PG or other degree programs.

Many professionals' mental health is gradually suffering as a result of their relentless pressure to be more, do more, and accomplish more. And it's not limited to medicine. Employees in corporate positions who are currently doing well might be pushed to take on more work or obtain more qualifications to remain relevant. Teachers' enthusiasm for teaching is frequently compromised by the expectation that they maintain up-to-date certifications. Even in family-run firms, the younger generation may feel tremendous pressure to expand the company beyond what has already been accomplished, losing sight of the initial delight that came from working in the family business. People's mental health is suffering in every industry as a result of this never-ending quest for "more."

A Call for Contentment

We need to reconsider this system. People's roles and contributions at every stage of their careers need to be valued. An MBBS should be regarded and valued for their work if they are performing it productively. Being "just" an MBBS should not be a source of guilt if it brings one contentment and joy. This holds true for all occupations. A teacher with a PhD is no more important than one who puts their all into the classroom without an additional degree. A company owner who operates a reliable, neighborhood store shouldn't feel less than someone who is branching out into other areas. Success is determined by how well we function in our current situation rather than by how much more we can do. We are the ones to change. The pressure to always strive for more will start to lessen when we learn to be happy with what we have and concentrate on living each day to the fullest. Only then will we be able to build a more balanced and healthy society where contentment and mental calmness are valued more highly than unending ambition.

Conclusion: In a society that is always pushing us to aim higher, it's critical to pause and consider whether the sacrifice is worthwhile. It's not always necessary to pursue the next certification or professional milestone to succeed. Being happy with what we have and doing our best in the roles we currently have can sometimes lead to true success. This statement is valid in all domains, including business, education, and medicine. By altering our perspective, we can discover genuine enjoyment in the here and now and lessen the crippling tension brought on by irrational social expectations. The definition of success has to be updated.

CHAPTER TEN

Preserving Dignity in Giving: A Reflection On Ethical Charity
Compassion and respect is important in charitable acts. There is a need to shift away from public displays that undermine the dignity of those in need.

Many people and families found themselves in need of basic necessities like food, shelter, and support during times of crisis like the COVID-19 lockdown. Many organizations and individuals stepped up in the spirit of humanity, providing aid where it was most needed. However, in a time when social media and public displays are prevalent, the practice of taking pictures of people getting aid has regrettably become more common, undermining the fundamental goal of charity.

I recently had a conversation with someone who shared a poignant experience. This person received food packets from officials distributing rations during the lockdown. A camera was quickly launched to record the event as the aid was given out. "Sir, I don't need this ration because you are taking my photo," the man said, graciously declining the assistance. He clarified that

the thought of being photographed while taking charity made him extremely uncomfortable. The long-term effects were the source of the worry rather than the present. "What if my kids are recruited in this very office one day after putting in a lot of effort and getting jobs, and that picture is on the wall? Would they not be embarrassed to believe that their father accepted alms, a kind of public "beek"? The conversation reveals a concerning trend. Giving, which is supposed to help people in need, is corrupted when it is used as a means of gaining attention from the public or for self-promotion. We deprive people of their dignity when we take pictures of them in their hour of need. In its purest form, charity ought to be about empathy, compassion, and a genuine desire to assist others rather than about obtaining praise or admiration. Self-respect and honour are intrinsically valued in our culture. Receiving charity is already a humiliating experience for many people, and the fear of being judged makes it considerably more difficult. These moments can become permanent signs of vulnerability when photographs are captured and possibly posted on social media or exhibited in public areas. The repercussions for recipients of charity might be extremely personal since they fear disgrace for themselves and their kids in the future. We need to consider if it is really necessary to record every instance of kindness. Giving is supposed to be a silent, heartfelt act that aims to elevate rather than degrade. We transform these actions into spectacles by snapping pictures, which puts the victim in a situation where their dignity is violated. This behaviour is a reflection of a larger social problem in which it is becoming difficult to distinguish between acts of self-interest and true compassion.

It is our duty as a society to protect the dignity of those who are less fortunate. Empathy must be the foundation of acts of compassion, and we must fight the impulse to draw attention to other people's hardships for our own or our organization's benefit. Remember that the silent satisfaction of seeing someone succeed without expecting praise is the real worth of contributing.

A person's dignity should never be traded for charity. Those who donate must be humble in their approach, realizing that their purpose is to provide assistance, not to draw attention to the suffering of others. Giving comes from the heart, not from the picture. Let's adopt a culture of silent charity, in which the influence we have on other people's lives rather than our social media feeds is the only testament to our generosity. This is about maintaining the moral foundation of our society, not just about personal sensitivity. Let our charitable deeds be recalled in the future for their kindness rather than the embarrassment they unintentionally cause.

CHAPTER ELEVEN

Adherence Is A Behavior: Do We Have The Right One?

Fundamentally, adherence is the practice of continuously abiding by laws, regulations, and promises. It is a conduct that exhibits accountability, self-control, and regard for accepted standards, it is more than just knowledge. Adherence governs our behavior in daily life and is not just applicable in legal or professional settings. Whether or not we apply what needs to be done to our lives is the question we need to ask ourselves, not if we realize it. To put it another way, are we acting wisely?

The gap between knowledge and action

Everyone in our society is familiar with the laws and regulations. We are familiar with workplace ethics, environmental regulations, traffic laws, and social manners. But knowing is not the same as doing. Adherence requires a deliberate attempt to match knowledge with behavior. Non-adherence frequently results from a desire for convenience over compliance, whether it be with regard to completing job commitments, managing garbage responsibly, or adhering to speed limits. The true difficulty Is in this gap between knowledge and action.

The consequences of non-adherence

Non-adherence has serious repercussions and is not a personal problem. A civilization cannot advance sustainably if fundamental rules are broken. Ignoring environmental regulations speeds up ecological degradation, disregarding traffic laws causes accidents, and disregarding ethical standards at work damages productivity and trust. Our quality of existence is shaped by our adherence to or lack thereof in every aspect of life.

Adherence in the health sector

Adherence is more than just a behavior in the medical field, it is a life-or-death situation. Every act of adherence, from patients following recommended treatment plans to medical personnel following procedures, has a direct impact on results. As a doctor employed at a Primary Health Centre (PHC), I have seen firsthand the impact that adherence or lack thereof has on public health. Simple but important advice, including completing antibiotic treatments or continuing immunizations, is frequently disregarded by patients. In the same way, to guarantee safety and effectiveness, healthcare personnel must follow standard treatment guidelines, reporting procedures, and infection control methods. In healthcare, adherence is more than just following procedures, it's also about fostering trust and guaranteeing accountability for improved health results. Cultivating the right behavior:Education, awareness, and encouragement are ways to promote adherence as a behavior. Although it starts on an individual basis, it flourishes in a setting that rewards and cherishes compliance. For instance, hospital hand hygiene or seatbelt programs have been successful when combined with positive reinforcement and visible role models. The secret to long-term behavioral change is to establish a culture that values adherence rather than disregards it.

A call to introspection

The question, "Do we have the right behavior?" forces us to reflect carefully. Do we always follow the rules, or do we only do so when it's convenient for us? Do we justify non-compliance, or are we genuinely responsible for our actions? Adherence is not about selective application; it is about embodying values and acting with integrity in all areas of life.

Conclusion

In conclusion, progress, safety, and trust in society are all based on adherence. It involves living in harmony with group objectives and duties rather than just abiding by the law. Promoting adherence as a fundamental behavior will help us close the knowledge gap and create a better future. The question still stands: Do we have the appropriate one, whether it's in the medical field, on the highways, or in day-to-day living?

CHAPTER TWELVE

Mouj (Mother): The Soul Of Humanity
A heartfelt tribute to mothers who, through their unconditional love and unyielding strength, illuminate the path of life for their children

The term "mother" (mouj in Kashmiri) expresses a profound emotion that even the most poetic language cannot convey. It is more than just a word; it is an emotion, a bond, and a whole realm of selfless giving and love. A mother's love transcends human comprehension, and her power, hidden behind a tender smile, is unrivalled. Over the years, I have written about mothers on several occasions, trying to express the magnitude of their contributions to our lives. Yet, despite my previous attempts, a recent experience in the labor room moved me so profoundly that I couldn't resist writing again about the unmatched greatness of a mother. In the course of my profession, I had the privilege of witnessing a moment that profoundly deepened my respect for mothers. While attending a normal delivery, I was struck by the raw, unfiltered power of a mother's love. The labor room echoed with the screams of a woman enduring unimaginable pain, her body Laboring through the process of bringing life into the world. Yet, amidst her suffering, a moment of pure maternal instinct took me by surprise. As soon as the baby was delivered before she even had a chance to acknowledge her own pain or exhaustion, her first words were, "How is the baby?" That single sentence spoke volumes. Here was a woman who had gone through excruciating pain, yet her first concern was not herself, but the life she had just brought into the world. That moment encapsulated the essence of motherhood love so selfless, so unconditional, that it prioritizes another life over its own. It is often said that paradise lies beneath the feet of mothers, and witnessing this scene made me understand why. A mother does not simply give birth; she nurtures, sacrifices, and endures for her child. From the moment of conception, her body becomes a vessel of creation. She shares her blood, her nutrients, and even her strength to ensure the survival of the tiny life growing inside her.

Pregnancy and childbirth are only the beginning of the journey of motherhood. What follows is a lifetime of sacrifices—sleepless nights, tireless days, and endless prayers for the well-being of her child. A mother doesn't measure her worth by her achievements but by the happiness and success of her children. Her strength is often silent, her sacrifices invisible, and her love immeasurable. In our fast-paced lives, we often take mothers for granted. Their unwavering presence becomes so routine that we fail to acknowledge their struggles and sacrifices. But we must remind ourselves that a mother's love is not an entitlement; it is a blessing. Every scar she bears, every wrinkle on her face, and every grey strand of her hair tells a story of her resilience and devotion.

As I reflect on the moment I witnessed in the labor room, I am filled with a deep sense of gratitude for the unsung heroes we call mothers. They are the ones who make homes out of houses, who turn tears into smiles, and who transform ordinary lives into extraordinary journeys.

To all the mothers out there: you are the silent warriors, the unsung poets of love, and the pillars of humanity. Your strength inspires us, your love heals us, and your sacrifices humble us. Let us not wait for a special occasion to celebrate mothers. Every day is an opportunity to express gratitude, to show kindness, and to honor the incredible role they play in our lives.

To my own mouj, and to all the mothers around the world, I bow to your strength, your love, and your endless sacrifices. You are the real heroes, the true nurturers of life, and the living embodiment of compassion. Thank you for everything you do, even when we fail to notice.

Conclusion

A mother's love is not just a feeling; it is a force that shapes the world. It is the reason we grow, the reason we thrive, and the reason we learn to love. Let us cherish this force, honour it, and never forget that behind every successful life stands a mother who believed, nurtured, and sacrificed.

CHAPTER THIRTEEN

Fathers: Silent architects of unseen foundations

I am dedicating this article to my dear Abu, a remarkable figure whose silent contributions have shaped the very fabric of our family's journey. In the tapestry of parental love, fathers often remain unsung heroes, and my Abu is no exception. With his unwavering support, sacrifices, and the profound love he has showered upon me from sending me abroad to fulfill my dream of becoming a doctor to ensuring every comfort and necessity, my father's sacrifices become the emotional core of our story. Join me in celebrating the silent architects—our fathers—who, through their selfless acts, create the unseen foundations of our lives. I love you, Abu.

In the narrative of familial love and sacrifices, the spotlight often gravitates towards mothers, and rightfully so. The journey from conception to birth is a remarkable one, with mothers nurturing life within their wombs for nine months. However, amidst the celebration of maternal love, the role of fathers is sometimes relegated to the shadows, despite their profound contributions.

A father's involvement begins well before a child takes their first breath. During the delicate stages of pregnancy, a father is the silent guardian, ensuring the well-being of both the expectant mother and the unborn child. From accompanying the mother to medical check-ups to providing unwavering support, fathers play a pivotal role in creating a conducive environment for a healthy pregnancy.

Post-birth, a father's responsibilities extend beyond the walls of the home. Stepping out to earn a living, fathers become the providers, ensuring that their children have not just the basic necessities, but a life of comfort and security. The selflessness of a father is evident in the sacrifices made, often choosing to go without to fulfill the needs and desires of the family.

A father becomes the unsung hero, the backbone of the family structure. Despite facing the challenges of the outside world, he remains resilient in his commitment to the well-being of his loved ones. The love of a father is showcased not only in grand gestures but in the everyday sacrifices that often go unnoticed.

In a world that sometimes overlooks the significant contributions of fathers, it becomes imperative to endorse and celebrate their love. Recognizing the enduring support, sacrifices, and unwavering dedication of a father enriches the tapestry of familial bonds. They are not just providers but architects shaping the unseen foundation that defines the strength and resilience of the family unit. It is a reminder that in the symphony of parenthood, both mothers and fathers harmonize to create a nurturing and loving environment for their children.

CHAPTER FOURTEEN

The Capitalist Trap: Where Love Is Replaced By Materialism

In the relentless pursuit of success, we've prioritized material gain over emotional well-being, leaving our children longing for connection

In the pursuit of success, we have turned into the worst type of capitalists, both in our personal and professional lives. We evaluate everything, even how we raise our kids, in terms of financial gain. We provide them the expensive gadgets, clothing, and educational opportunities, yet we neglect to teach them the most important lesson of life: love.

A Childhood of Material Promises

Securing their child's future in terms of money, job, and status is the obsession of today's parents. Children are taught from an early age to think that material possessions, not emotions, determine success. We lead kids to believe that high-end toys, branded shoes and lucrative careers are the keys to happiness. Emotional health, love, and care are subordinated. At home, people talk about their education, careers, and financial stability. We hardly ever ask our kids how they're feeling, what they're afraid of, or what makes them happy. As a reminder that the world is harsh and that only the fittest survive, we encourage kids to compete instead. Children grow up emotionally detached in this environment when warmth and affection take a backseat.

The Internet Becomes Their Best Friend

Children seek out company elsewhere when they don't feel emotionally cared for at home. They become their closest friends as a result of using their phones and the internet. The internet only provides an escape; unlike parents, it does not condemn, criticize, or set expectations. Their comfort zones, social media, online gaming, and virtual friendships fill the emotional void left by their families. They feel unloved and unheard at home. However, they discover listeners on the internet, even if such relationships are fleeting or occasionally damaging. This addiction to the digital world is a desperate attempt to find love, approval, and attention, it goes beyond simple amusement.

The Real Problem Isn't Screen Time, It's Capitalism

I just came across a Facebook discussion panel where individuals were discussing how to limit kids' screen use. They expressed concern about excessive use of mobile devices and the internet and offered remedies such as digital detoxes, time limits, and outside activities. However, I think they overlooked the true problem, which is capitalism itself. The majority of screen time conversations centre on symptoms rather than causes. People blame social media, technology, and even kids for becoming "addicted" to screens. However, we hardly ever inquire why kids are using screens in the first place.

The irony is that the same capitalist system that makes parents emotionally unavailable also profits from children's screen addiction. Tech companies design apps and games to keep children hooked, knowing that their loneliness will drive engagement. Schools and parents push digital learning tools but then complain about excessive screen exposure. The entire advertising industry thrives on making children dependent on virtual entertainment, feeding them endless distractions.

Instead of asking, "How can we reduce screen time?" we should ask, "How can we create a society where children don't feel the need to escape into screens?"

Even Marriage is a Business Deal

The obsession with material possessions is not limited to childhood, it permeates all phases of life, including marriage. When selecting a life partner for their children, parents today place a higher priority on financial stability than on love, compatibility, and understanding. As if love and respect were less important than income, parents frequently insist that their daughters marry a man who works for the government or has a steady salary. The ideal bride, according to sons, should bring wealth, prestige, or a strong family history. Marriage is reduced to a business agreement, despite the fact that it is meant to be a holy tie founded on friendship and trust.

As a result, many people enter unhappy marriages, bound by financial convenience rather than genuine emotional connection.

Then, when these marriages fail or become emotionally suffocating, we blame the younger generation for not knowing how to "adjust" rather than questioning the capitalist mindset that shaped these relationships.

Blaming the Children for Our Own Failures

Then, when these children grow up and start seeking affection elsewhere sometimes in the wrong places we blame them. When they turn to toxic relationships, addiction, or reckless behaviour in search of the love they never received at home, we label them as irresponsible. We fail to see that their actions are a desperate cry for the emotional fulfillment we denied them. We complain that children today are selfish, insensitive, or obsessed with social validation. But who made them this way? If all their lives they were told that success equals wealth and possessions, why should they suddenly believe in love, kindness, and morality? It's time to examine yourself. We must start making investments in emotional well-being rather than merely offering material comfort. Have a Conversation with Your Kids: not only about their education and grades, but also about their feelings, aspirations, and anxieties.

Make them feel heard. Teach Them the Value of Love: Demonstrate to them via actions that relationships, kindness, and inner serenity are just as important to pleasure as material wealth. The value of spending time with your child outweighs any costly present. More than your gifts, they need your presence. Rather than criticizing kids for spending too much time on screens, consider whether you have provided them an incentive to engage with people in person. Modify the Marriage Mindset: Seek out a life partner who shares your beliefs, respects you, and is emotionally compatible rather than one who is focused on money accounts and pay stubs. We must set an example for our children by prioritizing love over material possessions. Prove to them that connections are more important than money.

CHAPTER FIFTEEN

Navigating Ethical Boundaries in Kashmir's Media Landscape: A Call for Responsible Journalism and Content Creation

In the scenic valleys of Kashmir, the surge of individuals aspiring to become journalists and content creators has brought both vibrancy and challenges to the media landscape. While the desire to share stories is commendable, recent trends reveal a concerning disregard for ethical boundaries, impacting the quality and integrity of journalism and content creation in the region.

The Proliferation of Journalism and Content Creation

Kashmir has witnessed an influx of aspiring journalists and content creators eager to contribute to the digital narrative. However, this surge has led to a significant challenge—ethical breaches that compromise the very essence of responsible journalism and content creation.

One alarming trend is the disregard for individuals' privacy. Some journalists, in their pursuit of sensationalism, have resorted to revealing private details, often through videos and intrusive questioning. This erosion of privacy not only violates ethical standards but also undermines the trust between media professionals and the communities they serve.

Adding to the complexity is the rise of self-proclaimed journalists. Without adherence to established journalistic principles and accountability, these individuals contribute to the erosion of the credibility of journalism in Kashmir. The lack of oversight raises questions about the authenticity and reliability of the information being disseminated.

Similarly, content creators find themselves under scrutiny for over sharing and veering into sensationalism once their primary content is exhausted. This tendency to showcase aspects of life that cross ethical boundaries contributes to a narrative that lacks substance and responsibility.

Media organizations and regulatory bodies play a crucial role in upholding ethical standards. By establishing and enforcing guidelines, they can ensure that journalists adhere to principles that safeguard the integrity of their profession. Additionally, fostering a culture of accountability within the media community will contribute to a more responsible and transparent media environment.

In recent times, the picturesque region of Kashmir has found itself entangled in an unexpected controversy, not stemming from political unrest or social upheaval, but from an unforeseen realm – the world of YouTube content creators. A staggering scam of approximately 50 crores has sent shockwaves through the community, shedding light on the darker side of online content creation.

YouTube, a platform that has become synonymous with creativity, entertainment, and information, has also become a breeding ground for scams and fraudulent activities. In this particular case, a group of content creators operating in Kashmir stands accused of orchestrating a scheme that has left many victims in its wake.

The scam, which unfolded over a period of time, involved these You Tubers enticing viewers with promises of lucrative returns through dubious investment schemes. Using their influence and subscriber base, they managed to persuade unsuspecting individuals to part with significant sums of money. As the scale of the scam became apparent, authorities began to piece together the puzzle, leading to investigations and legal actions.

The impact of such scams extends beyond financial losses. The trust that viewers place in content creators as influencers and guides is eroded, leaving a sense of betrayal in its wake. This incident underscores the need for increased vigilance and regulatory measures within the online content creation space.

It is essential to recognize that the majority of content creators on platforms like YouTube operate with integrity, aiming to entertain, educate, and inspire their audiences. However, instances like this scam emphasize the potential for abuse of this influence and the responsibility that comes with it.

As the investigation unfolds, questions arise about the role of platforms like YouTube in monitoring and regulating content. While these platforms have community guidelines and reporting mechanisms, the sheer volume of content makes it challenging to police every video. Striking a balance between freedom of expression and protecting users from fraudulent activities remains an ongoing challenge.

Furthermore, this incident highlights the importance of digital literacy and awareness among viewers. Educating the audience about recognizing potential scams, verifying information, and approaching online content with a critical mindset is crucial to safeguard against such manipulative practices.

In the face of these challenges, there is an urgent need for a renewed commitment to ethical standards in journalism and content creation. Journalists must prioritize accuracy, fairness, and sensitivity, respecting the privacy and dignity of individuals even in the pursuit of a compelling story. Content creators, too, should exercise discretion, ensuring that their narratives contribute positively to the digital discourse.

The responsibility extends beyond media professionals to the audience. Empowering individuals to critically engage with the content they consume can create a demand for ethical reporting and content creation. Informed consumers play a vital role in shaping a media landscape that values integrity and responsibility.

Conclusion:

As Kashmir navigates the evolving dynamics of journalism and content creation, it stands at a crossroads. The choices made today will shape the narrative for generations to come. By championing ethical standards, respecting privacy, and fostering accountability, journalists and content creators can contribute to a media landscape that reflects the true spirit of Kashmir—a region of diverse stories, rich traditions, and resilient people.

CHAPTER SIXTEEN

Impact of Government Actions on Street Vendors

By understanding their struggles and advocating for empathetic, inclusive policies, we can work towards creating cities that thrive without leaving behind those who earn not for grand aspirations, but for the simple sustenance of their families

In the bustling streets of our cities, a significant segment of the population strives to make ends meet by engaging in activities like street vending. These individuals aren't seeking to amass wealth or construct towering buildings; their primary goal is more fundamental – putting food on the table for their families.

Unfortunately, these very individuals, often belonging to the economically disadvantaged, find themselves in the crosshairs of government actions. As cities evolve and regulations tighten, the plight of street vendors becomes increasingly precarious.

The recent viral video of an elderly man being forcefully dragged and witnessing his livelihood vandalized by government authorities is a stark reminder of the harsh realities faced by those who depend on street vending for survival. The emotional impact of such scenes is undeniable, as hearts burst into tears witnessing the struggles of individuals who simply seek to provide for their families. Street vendors play a vital role in the economic fabric of our cities, offering affordable goods and services while contributing to the vibrancy of local communities. However, as urban landscapes transform and governments implement stringent measures, these hardworking individuals often bear the brunt of the changes.

Understanding the Struggle

The men and women who set up shop on sidewalks and street corners aren't doing so out of choice but out of necessity. They form part of the informal economy, grappling with limited resources and opportunities. Their daily earnings are not earmarked for grand investments; instead, they are a lifeline, ensuring a modest meal for their children and loved ones.

The Unseen Impact

Government actions, ostensibly taken for urban development or regulatory compliance, can inadvertently exacerbate the challenges faced by these vulnerable groups. Vandalizing their meager inventory or imposing stringent restrictions may seem like necessary steps, but they fail to address the root causes of poverty and push these individuals further into hardship.

A Call for Empathy and Inclusive Policies

It is imperative to delve into the underlying reasons behind such government measures. Is there a way to strike a balance between urban development and safeguarding the livelihoods of those on the margins of society? Empathy must be a guiding principle in crafting policies that not only regulate but also uplift the lives of the economically disadvantaged.

Promoting Sustainable Solutions

Rather than punitive actions, governments should focus on comprehensive, inclusive policies that consider the socio-economic context. Providing alternative spaces, skill development programs, and financial assistance can be more constructive approaches. Collaborative efforts involving local communities, policymakers, and urban planners are essential to finding sustainable solutions that protect both the vibrancy of our cities and the livelihoods of the most vulnerable.

In conclusion, the dichotomy between urban development and the well-being of street vendors is a complex challenge. By understanding their struggles and advocating for empathetic, inclusive policies, we can work towards creating cities that thrive without leaving behind those who earn not for grand aspirations, but for the simple sustenance of their families.

CHAPTER SEVENTEEN

Understanding Sufism: A Guide To Spiritual Purification

The mystical form of Islam known as Sufism emphasizes spiritual enlightenment and internal purity.

Importance in the spiritual domain

It is of great significance as an instrument to gain a deeper understanding of spirituality and establish a closer relationship with Allah.

Reference to prominent Sufi scholars and their teachings

Prominent Sufi philosophers such as Rumi, Ibn Arabi, and Al-Ghazali placed great emphasis on the pursuit of divine love, self-awareness, and introspection. Maulana Rumi's quote, "The essence of Sufism is to search for the truth within yourself," sums up the philosophy of Sufism in a lovely way.

Examining the teachings of Hazrat Sultan Bahoo

The core of Hazrat Sultan Bahoo's teachings is that having a pure heart is essential to achieving spiritual enlightenment.

Emphasis on the importance of a pure heart

Sufis place great importance on heart purity, which transcends human recognition in favour of divine acceptance. The insightful statement made by Sultan Bahoo, "I am neither here nor there; I am in the love of the beloved," emphasizes the importance of heavenly love over earthly ties.

MYTHS REGARDING CONTEMPORARY SUFISM

Is the individual calling oneself a Sufi today a true Sufi?

The true essence of Sufism is often misinterpreted in modern perspectives. Making ostentatious rituals or appearances outside true Sufism is not important. Being a mystic or ascetic to get material prosperity is not the goal of Sufism. It does not entail acting contrary to Islamic principles or seeking attention by superficial acts of religiosity. Sadly, for some people, modern Sufism means dressing like a mystic, attending ostentatious rituals, and attempting to attract attention from others. Nevertheless, this is far from the central ideas of Sufism.

Common misconceptions about Sufism

A common misconception is that Sufism is primarily about ostentatious rituals and outward appearances, which are not true to its core principles. Resolving Misconceptions: Misconceptions about Sufism are exacerbated by false depictions of this spiritual path, such as materialism and superficial piety.

Qualities of an actual Sufi

A true Sufi reflects heavenly characteristics in their behaviour and manner, embodying moral purity, self-mastery, and empathy for all beings. Examples of Sufis in Different Roles: True Sufis display spiritual characteristics and deliver heavenly light through their behaviour, regardless of whether they are dressed in traditional or modern outfits. Sufism places a strong emphasis on moral purity, self-mastery, and empathy for people in need and without resources. These concepts lead people to a state of inner peace and spiritual awareness.

Methods for developing inner peace: Methods for achieving inner peace and spiritual enlightenment include meditation, dhikr (remembering God), and charitable deeds. Sufis use the analogy of a pure heart as a mirror reflecting holy light to represent the soul's relationship with the divine.

Sufi ideals: Examples: The unshakable commitment and selflessness of historical people like Sheikh ul Alam and Ameer Kabir serve as models of the Sufi values. These great Sufis demonstrated genuine spiritual devotion and should be an encouragement to everyone wishing to follow the Sufi path. Sheikh ulAlam's teachings: As routes to divine union, Sheikh ulAlam's teachings place a strong emphasis on spiritual discipline, humility, and service to humanity. Beyond philosophical bounds, he preached love and compassion, accepting all creatures as manifestations of the Divine.

Ameer Kabir's teachings: Ameer Kabir's teachings emphasized the importance of letting go of the ego in order to achieve spiritual enlightenment and the transformational power of love. His life was devoted to serving others and promoting the message of divine love and unity, making him the epitome of humility and selflessness. Sultan Abdul Hamid II's role: Despite wearing coats and pants, Sultan Abdul Hamid II, the last Ottoman Empire ruler, is seen as a modern Sufi figure. He dressed in contemporary fashion while maintaining a close relationship with Allah. His example serves as a reminder that honesty and dedication are found in the heart and that appearances do not define one's spiritual connection. A fascinating aspect of Sultan Abdul Hamid II's character is his Sufi inclination, which combines traditional spirituality with the requirements of modern governance. He was the head of state in the Ottoman Empire, but he remained deeply rooted in Islamic spirituality and Sufi teachings. Inner Connection with Allah: Abdul Hamid II's personal devotion to Allah and his adherence to Islamic teachings were indicative of his Sufi personality. He maintained his spiritual roots and turned to prayer, meditation, and introspection for direction and comfort despite the luxuries of modern life and power.

THE ACTUAL SUFI PATH

Preventing misinterpretations :It is vital to stay clear from misinterpretations regarding Sufism, acknowledging that it is not a strategy for obtaining commercial or individual benefit.

Emphasis on selflessness and inner development: The authentic Sufi path leads people toward spiritual satisfaction by emphasizing selflessness, inner development, and devotion to the Divine. Value of Virtue Cultivation: Developing virtues such as humility, love, and compassion is essential to the Sufi path because it promotes spiritual development and union with the Divine.

Call for genuine devotion: People are guided toward spiritual enlightenment and inner serenity by genuine devotion and commitment to the spiritual path. Sufism emphasizes spiritual awareness, personal purification, and connection to the Divine as a timeless route to enlightenment.

Reminder of the significance of spiritual purity: People can go on a life-changing path towards divine harmony and spiritual fulfillment by practising virtues and spiritual purity.

Urge to adopt core principles: In order to experience greater spiritual fulfillment, personal development, and a closer relationship with God, let's embrace the fundamental principles of Sufism.

CHAPTER EIGHTEEN

The Chameleon Faces of Politics in Kashmir

A Tale of Betrayal and Forgotten Wounds

With a complex netting of regional, national, and international interests, Kashmir's political arena has long been volatile. Due to the region's special geopolitical significance, politicians frequently have to modify their strategies to negotiate the shifting sands of power, making it a hotspot of conflict.

Past Developments Affecting Politics in Kashmir

The political history of Kashmir is filled with disputes and conflict. The area has had decades of instability, from the 1947 division of India to the late 20th-century insurgency movements. Political plotting by regional and outside actors has influenced the future of Kashmir and its people.

The People's Suffering: The Kashmiri people have been suffering from the worst of the political unrest for many generations. The Kashmiri people have faced severe hardships, including human rights violations and curfews, which have been enforced. There have been casualties, displaced people, and a generalized feeling of unease as a result of the ongoing conflict.

Voting patterns and forgotten wounds: The people of Kashmir frequently find themselves in an ironic situation during elections, notwithstanding the traumas inflicted upon them. Promises of a brighter future may cause the memory of past atrocities to vanish. The need for justice can occasionally be compromised by compulsion, financial benefits, and the need for stability. The phenomenon known as *"forgetting suffering"* has several reasons why people in Kashmir tend to forget their past traumas. Even in the middle of hardship, people can frequently adjust to their circumstances due to their innate resilience. Furthermore, the constant onslaught of political discourse and propaganda can potentially cover up communal memory and the true scope of historical injustices. Furthermore, people may choose to emphasise positivity above the resentment of the past as a result of the appeal of hope and the promise of a better future overshadowing the traumas of the past.

Political personalities' resilience: The ability of Kashmiri political personalities to hold onto power despite their deeds is proof of their stubbornness. These people may confront the very people they have mistreated by using a combination of charm, deceit, and force. It speaks volumes about the nature of politics in Kashmir and how people can adapt to and live in such a turbulent environment. It's common knowledge in Kashmir's complicated political landscape that politicians fight for positions of authority not always to represent the interests of the people but rather to grow their own. The goals of the people and the acts of their elected officials are at odds because of this self-serving style of governance. Instead of serving as platforms for real change, political fights end up serving as battlefields for factional advantage.

Opportunism in Kashmiri Politics: People and organizations frequently take advantage of the unstable atmosphere in Kashmir for their gain. Opportunism has long been a defining feature of Kashmiri politics. Opportunists thrive in the instability of Kashmiri politics, whether through allying with powerful interest groups, taking advantage of socio-political tensions, or obtaining outside help. This selfish mindset creates an endless loop of instability as special interests keep influencing politics to suit their interests, frequently at the expense of the general public. It's a lamentable reality that the people of Kashmir are often caught in the web of political exploitation, manipulated by false promises and relentless propaganda. As we reflect on the cyclical nature of our political landscape, it becomes imperative for us to reflect and question how we can break free from this cycle of deceit. We yearn for a Kashmir where genuine peace and prosperity prevail, and where the aspirations of the people are not sacrificed at the altar of political expediency. It's time to shift our focus from transient political figures to enduring solutions. *Let us come together as a community to seek answers, to demand accountability, and to forge a path towards a brighter future. Politicians may come and go, but the underlying issues persist. It's up to us, the people of Kashmir, to reclaim our agency, challenge the status quo, and strive towards building a society where true justice, equality, and peace reign supreme. Only then can we truly hope to see Kashmir become the peaceful heaven we all deserve.*

CHAPTER NINETEEN

The Lost Conscience: A Reflection on Our Actions

In the contemporary world, it is increasingly apparent that, as Muslims, we are losing touch with our conscience and moral responsibilities. The dissonance between our actions and the plight of our brothers and sisters in Palestine is a stark reminder of this troubling reality.

Celebrating Amidst Suffering

Our brothers and sisters in Palestine, on the other side of the world, go through terrible pain and fight every day just to survive. They struggle with loss, live in continual danger, and try to meet their fundamental needs. Meanwhile, we observe festivities characterized by firecrackers and partying in other regions of the world, including our own towns. This striking difference draws attention to a serious break from the empathy and togetherness that Islam instills in us. While Eid celebrations are a time for happiness and connection, the core of these teachings is contradicted by participating in extravagant celebrations and firecrackers. Islam calls us to rejoice in community, humility, and thankfulness, but how can we truly celebrate when our fellow

Muslims are suffering?

The Scene In Pulwama: A Heartbreaking Reality

Scenes from Pulwama that I saw recently broke my heart. These celebrations showed how far we have strayed from the path of empathy and compassion. As our Palestinian brothers and sisters suffer, we seem blind, wasting our time and energy on actions that are wasteful and indifferent to the suffering that surrounds us. The noise and spectacle of firecrackers may provide a brief sense of joy, but they also reflect a deeper disregard for the struggles of others, reflecting a loss of the very compassion that Islam calls us to uphold.

A Call For Respect And Solidarity

While we might not be able to help directly the Palestinian people, we nevertheless owe it to them to understand and stand in solidarity with those innocent people. Our interests and principles are reflected in our actions—or lack thereof. Our faith as Muslims requires us to show compassion, raise awareness, and give prayers in support of those who are in need. As Kashmiris, we are falling short in every way when it comes to defending the values of humanity and Islam. We must never forget that our moral obligations should always take precedence over our festivities. We need to shift our focus from mindless festivities to real gestures of solidarity and support for those who are suffering.

Parental Responsibility: The Foundation Of Moral And Religious Behavior

The role of parents in shaping the moral and religious behavior of their children cannot be overstated. Unfortunately, many parents today seem more concerned with providing food and clothes than with instilling the values of Islam in their children. Material comfort is important, but it is not enough. Parents should strive to be friends with their children, engaging them in conversations about their daily activities and friendships. This friendly approach encourages children to share their thoughts and experiences openly, creating an environment where moral and ethical discussions can flourish.

Parents must take an active role in teaching their children about Islam, the teachings of the Prophet Muhammad (peace be upon him), and the wisdom of the Awliya (saints). They should emphasize the importance of good behavior, as parents are the first and most influential teachers in a child's life. By fostering a deep understanding of Islamic teachings and principles, parents can guide their children towards a path of empathy, compassion, and moral integrity. Teaching children about the values of kindness, respect, and solidarity can help them grow into conscientious individuals who are aware of their responsibilities towards others. It is our responsibility as Muslims to look into our behaviour and correct it to be more in line with Islamic principles. Rather than participating in careless festivities, we should foster empathy and a sense of solidarity with those who are suffering. By establishing moral principles in their children and pointing them in the direction of righteousness, parents play a critical part in this process. We can only hope to recover our lost conscience and fully live out the teachings of our faith if we deeply integrate Islamic teachings into our lives and the lives of our children. By making this deliberate effort, we can honour our faith and solidarity while transforming our festivities into heartfelt displays of thankfulness and unity.

CHAPTER TWENTY

Climate Change Is A Health Crisis
Examining the impact, vulnerabilities and mitigation strategies and protecting human health amidst environmental challenges

Once an unknown threat, climate change is now an urgent reality that affects every aspect of our lives, including our health. This article discusses into the complex relationship between human health and climate change, examining its sources, indications, effects, vulnerable groups, and mitigation efforts.

Understanding Climate Change

Long-term changes in temperature, precipitation patterns, and other atmospheric parameters are referred to as climate change, and they are mostly brought on by human activity such as the burning of fossil fuels, deforestation, and industrial activities.

The Reasons Behind Climate Change

The interplay of natural processes and human activity leads to climate change. While natural occurrences like solar radiation fluctuations and volcanic eruptions do play a part, human-caused factors like greenhouse gas emissions and altered land use are the main causes.

Climate Change Indicators

Rising temperatures, melting ice caps, altered precipitation patterns, and an increase in the frequency of extreme weather events like heatwaves, droughts, and storms are all signs of climate change.

Effect on the Well-Being of Humans

Air Pollution

Across the globe, air pollution poses a serious health risk and is made worse by climate change. It originates from a number of sources, such as burning biomass, industrial activity, and vehicle emissions. Nitrogen dioxide (NO_2) and fine particulate matter ($PM2.5$) are the main pollutants linked to lung cancer and respiratory conditions like asthma and chronic obstructive pulmonary disease (COPD). Furthermore, the combination of sunlight and pollution produces ground-level ozone, which aggravates respiratory disorders and advances cardiovascular illnesses.

Allergens

Asthma and respiratory allergies become worse by rising temperatures and changing weather patterns, which alter the distribution and quantity of mold spores and allergenic pollen. Longer and more intense pollen seasons expose susceptible people to higher allergen concentrations for longer periods of time. Furthermore, the timing of pollen release is altered by alterations in plant phenology brought about by climate change, making allergy management and treatment more difficult.

Impacts on Water Quality

A number of mechanisms, such as modified precipitation patterns, elevated temperatures, and adjustments to runoff and sedimentation, are all impacted by climate change. These elements have the potential to contaminate water sources with chemicals, diseases, and harmful algal blooms (HABs). Waterborne cholera is a serious health danger during major weather events and flooding because it grows in warm, stagnant waterways. In a similar vein, HABs generate toxins that can contaminate drinking water and have a negative impact on health, including neurological problems and liver damage.

Impacts on Water and Food Supplies

The disruption of water and food supply chains caused by climate change puts food security and nutrition at risk. Unpredictable precipitation patterns, protracted droughts, and a lack of water limit crop yields and agricultural productivity, which, especially in disadvantaged communities, results in food shortages and hunger. In addition, extreme weather events like storms and floods exacerbate food insecurity by destroying crops, contaminating food supply, and upsetting distribution networks. These health conditions are also more likely to cause diarrheal diseases and other watery infections.

Severe Weather

As a result of climate change, extreme weather events are becoming more frequent and dangerous for people's health and safety. Heat waves make heat-related disorders like heat exhaustion and heatstroke more common, especially among susceptible groups including the elderly, small children, and outdoor laborers. Hurricanes, tornadoes, and cyclones are examples of severe storms that can inflict fatalities, bodily harm, and mental health problems like depression and post-traumatic stress disorder (PTSD). Heavy rainfall-related flooding and landslides uproot communities, interfere with the provision of basic services, and accelerate the spread of diseases that are transmitted through the water.

Degradation of the Environment

Degradation of the environment is caused by climate change and results in habitat loss, a decrease in biodiversity, and disruption of ecosystems. Due to changes in land use and resource extraction, deforestation weakens ecosystem resilience and puts populations at risk of natural disasters like floods and landslides. Pollination, disease control, water purification, and other ecosystem functions are all hampered by biodiversity loss, endangering human health and welfare. In addition to increasing health disparities and disproportionately harming vulnerable populations, environmental degradation also exacerbates social and economic inequality.

Unpredictable and Inconsistent Weather Change

Unpredictable and Inconsistent weather patterns, a hallmark of climate change, provide serious obstacles to food security and agriculture. Unseasonal frosts, extended droughts, and erratic rainfall interfere with crop growth cycles, alter planting schedules, and lower yields, which jeopardizes food supply and nutrition. Farmers have to adapt their agricultural operations and pest management techniques as a result of the increasing demands posed by pests and diseases brought on by unpredictable weather. Crop failures and lower harvests can also result in reduced food prices, social unrest, and economic problems, which exacerbates food insecurity and health inequities.

Groups of Vulnerable Populations: Climate change disproportionately affects some groups of people, such as the elderly, children, residents of low-income areas, and people with pre-existing medical disorders.

Developing Capabilities in the Community

Giving communities the information and tools they need to lessen the negative effects of climate change on their health is essential. This involves putting in place early warning systems for severe weather and encouraging adaptable tactics to reduce health hazards.

People have the ability to protect their health from the effects of climate change by being proactive. This entails leading a sustainable lifestyle, enhancing the quality of the air indoors, drinking enough of water during heat waves, and being ready for anything.

Conclusion

To sum up, climate change is a serious hazard to human health that will have a significant impact on people's lives, communities, and international health systems. In order to create resilience and safeguard the health and well-being of present and future generations, addressing this issue necessitates swift action at all levels, from individual behaviour adjustments to policy initiatives.

CHAPTER TWENTY-ONE

Proactive Health: Your Responsibility, Your Future

Your greatest asset is your health, which you have an obligation to safeguard. Make the first move toward a happier, healthier future today.

The key to a happy and successful life is good health. It's a treasure that needs to be looked after and safeguarded. We frequently disregard our health, putting it on the back burner during the daily bustle. Nevertheless, we owe it to ourselves to take care of our well-being; it is not only a choice. By taking proactive measures to maintain our health, we can avoid many illnesses and conditions and live longer and happier lives.

Get screened and save yourself from diseases and disorders

Regular check-ups are essential. They serve as an early warning system, identifying possible health concerns before they develop into more significant ones. Blood tests, annual check-ups and targeted screenings according to age and risk factors can detect diseases like diabetes, hypertension, and some malignancies early on, when they are most susceptible to treatment. You offer yourself the best chance of safeguarding good health and identifying any problems early by keeping up with these screenings.

Important questions to consider

It's critical to understand your risk factors. Consider these questions for a time:

Do you have a family history of high blood pressure or diabetes? Your health risks are significantly influenced by your family history. A more individualized and successful health plan can be created by you and your doctor using the knowledge of your family's medical history. Do you have a weight problem? Being overweight raises your chances of heart disease, diabetes, and some types of cancer, among other illnesses. A balanced diet and regular exercise are crucial for keeping a healthy weight. Do you have an age over thirty? Our bodies change as we get older, which can raise our chance of developing health problems. As we become older, routine tests and leading a healthy lifestyle become even more important. Do you smoke or drink alcohol? The use of tobacco and alcohol is a significant risk factor for many health issues, such as heart disease, lung cancer, and liver illness. Your health can be considerably improved by cutting back on or giving up these practices.

Risk factors

The first and most important step in preventing disease is identifying risk factors. These consist of lifestyle decisions, environmental exposures, genetic predispositions, and additional medical disorders. Your chance of experiencing major health problems can be greatly decreased by being aware of and taking action against these risks

Warning signs

Observe your body. Unusual pain, prolonged exhaustion, changes in skin tone, or unexplained weight loss are examples of symptoms that may be early indicators of more serious illnesses. Don't disregard these symptoms; get medical help right now.

Balanced diet is the key to a healthy lifestyle

A healthy diet must be well-balanced. It helps avoid chronic diseases and gives your body the nutrients it needs to function properly. Make an effort to include a range of whole grains, fruits, vegetables, lean meats, and healthy fats in your meals. Stay away of processed meals, sugar, and salt in excess.

Why wait for tomorrow? Take the first step towards a healthy life today

The delay can pose a serious obstacle to good health. Now is the ideal moment to begin caring for your health. Make reasonable, achievable adjustments that suit your way of life. Every step matters, whether it's arranging that overdue checkup, beginning a new workout regimen, or choosing better foods. In summary, your greatest asset is your health, which you have an obligation to safeguard. You may take charge of your health by being proactive, scheduling routine screenings, being aware of your risk factors, and eating a balanced diet. Avoid waiting for an alarm to go off. Make the first move toward a happier, healthier future today.

CHAPTER TWENTY-TWO

Beyond the classroom: The unseen burdens of teachers in Kashmir

Teachers are primarily entrusted with the noble task of educating future generations, guiding students through their prescribed syllabus, and fostering an environment conducive to learning. However, in Kashmir, teachers find themselves entangled in a web of responsibilities far removed from their primary role. This multifaceted burden not only undermines their professional dignity but also diverts their focus from their core educational duties.

Beyond the Classroom: Unseen Burdens

The main work of a teacher is to teach students their prescribed syllabus. Yet, in Kashmir, teachers have become "kathputli" manipulated into performing tasks unrelated to education. They are regularly deployed for other duties, compelled to manage administrative functions, and often assigned various other roles beyond the realm of teaching.

Teachers in Kashmir are frequently called upon to conduct surveys for government schemes, collect data for various administrative purposes, and even participate in non-academic training sessions. These duties consume a significant portion of their time, leaving them with less energy and enthusiasm for their primary teaching responsibilities.

One glaring example of this misplaced priority is the mandate requiring teachers to be present in schools even when students are at home. Recently, a two-day holiday was announced for students, but teachers were still required to attend school. This begs the question: What productive work can teachers accomplish in an empty school?

Another instance of this inefficiency is the imposition of extended school hours. Schools in the region announced morning timings from 8 AM to 1 PM, yet teachers were instructed to stay until 2 PM. With students gone, teachers are left with idle time, questioning the rationale behind this policy. If teachers are to remain in school, they should be assigned meaningful tasks that contribute to their primary role in education.

The Impact on Teaching

The additional responsibilities imposed on teachers inevitably distract them from their main task of teaching. When teachers are bogged down with non-educational duties, their energy, time, and focus are diluted. This not only affects the quality of education students receive but also dampens the morale of teachers who enter the profession with a passion for teaching.

Teachers are forced to juggle their teaching duties with administrative work, often resulting in increased stress and burnout. The pressure to meet administrative deadlines while maintaining the standard of teaching can lead to a decrease in overall job satisfaction and effectiveness. Moreover, the constant diversion from their core duties can hinder their professional growth and development, as they have less time to engage in activities that enhance their teaching skills.

Then, there is the issue of student performance. Critics often question why children in government schools do not excel academically. The answer lies in the fact that their teachers are preoccupied with non-teaching tasks, leaving little time for lesson planning, student engagement, and personalized instruction. The diversion of teachers' attention from their primary role severely impacts the quality of education that students receive.

A Call for Change

The government must reconsider these policies and streamline the duties of teachers to focus solely on teaching. By relieving teachers of extraneous tasks, the education system can enhance the quality of instruction and ensure that teachers can dedicate their full attention to the intellectual and personal development of their students.

Additionally, it is crucial to establish clear boundaries and guidelines regarding the roles and responsibilities of teachers. Providing them with support staff for administrative tasks and ensuring that non-teaching duties do not interfere with their primary role can help in creating a more focused and efficient educational environment.

In conclusion, teachers in Kashmir must be empowered to focus on their primary role of educating students. Authorities must recognize and address these issues to foster a more effective and fulfilling educational environment for both teachers and students. By prioritizing the core duties of teachers and minimizing non-teaching tasks, we can pave the way for a brighter future for the education system in Kashmir.

CHAPTER TWENTY-THREE

Doctors Are Humans Too: The Untold Challenges of the Medical Profession

The medical profession is one of the most respected and challenging fields in the world. Yet, despite the immense responsibility and dedication required, doctors often find themselves at the receiving end of undue criticism and mistreatment. It's crucial to remember that doctors too, are humans capable of feeling pain, stress, and exhaustion.

The Recent Tragic Incident

A horrific episode regarding the brutal murder and sexual assault of a postgraduate resident doctor recently shocked the medical community. The safety and well-being of doctors, who are often seen as unbreakable entities rather than weak people, are significant issues of discussion that have been brought up by this horrific incident. These kinds of incidents not only bring attention to the physical risks that doctors endure but also expose the lack of empathy and respect that they receive.

Misconceptions About Doctors

It is not unusual to hear people criticize doctors everywhere you go. Some call them arrogant, while others think that doctors are their servants and must treat them no matter what. Doctors are subjected to enormous expectations from patients and their families, who frequently want instant care and overlook the fact that doctors are human too. Even a five-minute wait might create a ruckus in a hospital. "Where is the doctor?" people insist to know. What's causing his lateness?" However, why do we assume that medical professionals are superhuman, constantly available, and never tired? In actuality, doctors are human beings with needs for relaxation and recovery time, just like any other machine.

Personal Experience In The Emergency Department

I remember an instance that happened in the ER where between 200 and 300 patients were waiting to be seen. A man came up to me in the middle of the confusion, furious that his patient had not received any attention. He began yelling at me even after I told him that we were trying our hardest to handle the excessive amount of cases. This is only one example; daily, many doctors deal with similar situations, if not worse. Videos depicting doctors being careless are all over the internet, but the people making the videos barely bother to think about how much work and stress doctors have daily. Is it so awful to take a five-minute break as a doctor?

The Need for Legal Protection

Adequate legal action must be taken to address the increasing anti-medical sentiment. Strict regulations need to be in place to guarantee that doctors feel secure and protected while carrying out their responsibilities. How can we expect doctors to give back to society to the fullest extent possible in the absence of a safe workplace?

Increased Security Is Needed, Particularly For Female Doctors

The lack of proper security in hospitals puts female doctors at serious risk, especially while working night shifts. They are more likely to experience harassment and assault when they are alone or have to navigate dimly lit corridors. Hospitals need to put their patients' safety first by putting stronger security measures in place, like round-the-clock security guards, secure transit, and rapid response systems. It is crucial to create a safe workplace so that medical professionals can concentrate on their work without worrying about their own safety.

Conclusion

Doctors undoubtedly have a responsibility to work with honesty and dedication, but society also has a responsibility to treat them with the respect and understanding they deserve. After all, a doctor is also a human—imperfect, yet striving to make a difference in the lives of others.

CHAPTER TWENTY-FOUR

My journey to Ladakh's enchanting wonders

As a proud Kashmiri, I recently embarked on a journey to Ladakh, a region renowned for its breathtaking landscapes and unique experiences. One of the first destinations that captivated my senses was Nubra Valley, where the mesmerizing Hunder sand dunes unfold, providing a stunning backdrop for encounters with double-humped camels. The sheer beauty of Ladakh left me in awe.

Beyond the picturesque scenery, Ladakh unveiled a different way of life. The harsh winter conditions painted a stark contrast to the familiar comforts of home. In Ladakh, water freezes in tanks during winter, making simple tasks like using the washroom a challenging endeavour. The need to manually fetch water in buckets highlighted the preciousness of this resource, a stark reminder of its scarcity in the region during winter.

Taking a bath in Ladakh's winter requires effort too. Burning wood to heat water becomes a ritual, emphasizing the importance of warmth and the struggle for basic amenities. These experiences served as a profound lesson, shedding light on the resilience and adaptability of the people living in such harsh conditions.

This journey outside my comfort zone brought a deeper understanding of life's essentials, particularly the value of accessible water. It underscored the privileges often taken for granted and instilled a newfound appreciation for the conveniences we enjoy in the comfort of our homes.

In the heart of Ladakh, where winter temperatures plunge below -15 degrees Celsius, the locals have devised ingenious ways to combat the bone-chilling cold. One remarkable aspect of their resilience lies in the use of fireplaces to warm their homes. This traditional method not only adds warmth to the rooms but also symbolizes the enduring spirit of the people who call this harsh landscape their home.

In essence, Ladakh not only offered breathtaking landscapes but also became a classroom of life lessons. It taught me that venturing beyond familiar territories opens doors to a world of experiences, challenges, and a deeper appreciation for the intricacies of daily life. Ladakh's raw beauty and the resilience of its people make it a destination not only for exploration but also for introspection.

CHAPTER TWENTY-FIVE

Unsung Heroes Of Ladakh: Serving In The Most Challenging Terrains
Regardless of its breathtaking beauty, Ladakh is a place with numerous challenging issues The terrible reality of isolated villages, harsh climates, and inaccessible terrains hides behind the magnificent mountains and serene monasteries. As a doctor posted in Kargil, I've had the honour of travelling throughout Ladakh, which has allowed me to deeply understand the lives of those who provide healthcare in these isolated areas. I recently visited several medical facilities in the most remote areas of Ladakh as a District Assessor for the National Quality Assurance Standards (NQAS). These visits demonstrated not only the difficulties but also the extraordinary commitment of our medical personnel, who operate under such difficult circumstances.

The Tough Journey to Pachari Sub-Centre
My visit to Pachari Sub-Centre, which is situated in a remote location with dangerously winding and small roads, stands out as one of my most unforgettable experiences. Since the route included negotiating risky roads with sheer cliffs on one side and no margin for error, arriving at Pachari itself seemed like an accomplishment. Arriving in Pachari was like travelling back in time. There were no mobile networks, internet access, or other modern conveniences that many of us take for granted. The local population was receiving essential medical services from the healthcare personnel stationed there in spite of these circumstances. It was very inspiring how determined they were to help despite having few resources and being so isolated.

Winners Beyond Standards
After finally reaching Pachari, I found myself wondering what there was to assess for NQAS. These healthcare workers were already winners in my heart, irrespective of whether they met the prescribed standards or had the required facilities. Their sheer commitment to providing care under such circumstances far outweighed any technical evaluation. To me, their

dedication itself was the highest standard one could achieve.

A Critical Need for Basic Infrastructure

I want to stress that although it is admirable that our healthcare system has reached such far-flung places, it is crucial to consider if these facilities are prepared to deal with emergencies. Basic infrastructure and emergency supplies are lacking in many of these sub-centres. Above all, every remote sub-centre should have at least one ambulance on duty. The ability to transfer a patient To a higher-level facility in the event of a medical emergency can make the difference between life and death.

A Lesson in Dedication and Resilience

I became aware of the obvious differences between working conditions in urban regions and these isolated places after visiting places like Pachari. In addition to being professionals, the medical staff here are vital to the communities they serve. They put in endless hours of effort, frequently without the luxury of quick aid or backup support, but they never fail in their commitment to their duties. I was deeply impacted by this encounter. I learned that commitment has no limits, and that motivated me to work even harder in my own line of work. It also emphasized the necessity of improved support networks for these medical professionals.

The need for recognition and support

In places like Pachari, the work of medical personnel is frequently underestimated. Even though their contributions are priceless, they hardly ever get the credit they deserve. Policymakers and higher authorities must try to visit these facilities. Simply showing the personnel that their work is appreciated and acknowledged can have a significant positive impact on their mood. Enhancing the infrastructure, resources, and incentives available to these remote centres can also have a big impact. Since they constitute the foundation of the local healthcare system and guarantee that even the most isolated populations have access to medical treatment, healthcare professionals in these locations shouldn't feel alone or unsupported.

Conclusion

The medical professionals assigned to Ladakh's difficult regions, like Pachari, are brave, committed, and resilient. Their efforts serve as a reminder of the value of service and a monument to the resilience of the human spirit. We owe them as a society not just our appreciation but also our assistance in enhancing the sustainability and fulfillment of their hard work. The steadfast attitude of the people of Ladakh, particularly the unsung heroes who give their lives to serve under the most difficult circumstances, is just as beautiful as the region's natural beauty. Since they are the real ambassadors of care and hope in this isolated area, it is our collective duty to make sure their efforts are acknowledged and encouraged.

CHAPTER TWENTY-SIX

Hard Work And Dedication Can Make A Change

A personal account of the remarkable changes achieved at the Primary Health Centre in Kargil, Ladakh through collective efforts and a commitment to excellence.

I have had an opportunity to work at the Primary Health Centre Shargole in the Kargil district of Ladakh for the last six months. During that time, I have witnessed firsthand the transformation that can be achieved through perseverance, hard work, and cooperation. Our entire staff has been working tirelessly to prepare for the upcoming National Quality Assurance Standards (NQAS) inspection, and the changes we've seen are remarkable.

The working atmosphere was different, and the challenges seemed overwhelming when I initially joined. However, today I see a renewed enthusiasm, a rejuvenated approach to work, and a collective dedication to excellence. Every aspect of the PHC, from improved patient care to more efficient workflows, tells a story of progress. Even though the changes are small, they have a significant impact—much like a mountain climber's steady steps that lead closer to the summit with every step.

The power of teamwork

Our growth has been the result of our collective efforts rather than any single achievement. True transformation in a health system can only occur when everyone within it is committed to the same goal. The staff at PHC Shargole has demonstrated exceptional cooperation, from the BMO and medical officers to the nursing staff and even the housekeeping team. When everyone's contribution matters, even the smallest flaws are accounted for in the system. Collaboration and mutual support are, therefore, essential. The unit as a whole may suffer from one person's mistake, but when everyone works together, the results are evident.

Going beyond the call of duty

What truly inspires me is the willingness of our staff to go beyond their designated roles. Employees here aren't confined to their specific duties. For instance, our dental assistant has taken on responsibilities well beyond the realm of medicine, acting as our unofficial plumber and electrician when needed. It's moments like these that demonstrate the extraordinary level of commitment our employees possess. They aren't just performing their duties; they are making a bigger difference by ensuring that our PHC runs efficiently at all times.

Dedication beyond certificates

As the NQAS assessment draws near, one thing is clear: whether or not we receive the NQAS certificate is secondary. What truly matters is the heart and dedication with which our staff has worked. Their commitment to improving the PHC is commendable, and no certificate can adequately capture the spirit of cooperation and perseverance they have shown. Regardless of the outcome, what is most important is the daily teamwork and dedication we've witnessed.

Conclusion

Ultimately, our contributions to PHC Shargole go beyond superficial changes. They reflect a shift in commitment, attitude, and unity. As we prepare for the NQAS evaluation, I am confident that this centre will continue to flourish and grow, thanks to the relentless efforts of everyone involved. After all, hard work transforms not just places but people, creating something enduring in the process.

CHAPTER TWENTY-SEVEN

Contrasting work cultures: A Tale of Kashmir and Ladakh

In the northern region lies a tale of two distinct cultures, each bearing its unique imprint on the work ethos and societal fabric. Kashmir and Ladakh, though geographically adjacent, present striking differences in their approach to work, bureaucracy, and interpersonal interactions.

Having experienced life in Kashmir firsthand, one notices a prevalent mentality characterized by bureaucracy laden with delays and a palpable air of ego among employees. Obtaining a simple certificate or navigating bureaucratic procedures often feels akin to navigating a labyrinth, with individuals being redirected from one department to another, only to be met with the refrain of "come tomorrow." From the lowest-ranked peon to the highest-ranking officials, ego appears to reign supreme, manifesting in reluctance to offer assistance or guidance to those seeking it. Inquiring about the simplest of matters can sometimes be met with curt responses or, at times, no response at all, leaving citizens feeling frustrated and disillusioned.

Conversely, the terrain changes dramatically as one ventures into Ladakh, where efficiency and a refreshing lack of ego characterize the work culture. Here, the swift disposal of tasks is not an anomaly but rather the norm. Obtaining necessary documents or completing bureaucratic procedures is a far more streamlined affair, often requiring just a day or two. What truly sets Ladakh apart, however, is the demeanor of its inhabitants. Grounded, humble, and inherently helpful, Ladakh is embody a sense of civility that transcends mere education or social status. Interactions with locals are marked by warmth, cooperation, and a genuine eagerness to assist fellow community members.

Indeed, the disparity in work cultures between Kashmir and Ladakh is not merely a matter of administrative efficiency but reflects deeper societal attitudes and values. While Kashmir grapples with the weight of bureaucratic red tape and inflated egos, Ladakh stands as a beacon of efficiency, humility, and community spirit. As we reflect on these contrasting narratives, it becomes evident that the essence of civilization lies not solely in education or technological advancement but in the way we treat one another and conduct ourselves in our daily interactions.

The people of Ladakh: A study in humility and unity

Ladakh often known as the "Land of High Passes" is well known for its incredibly beautiful natural surroundings and amazing landscapes. Ladakh, a geological wonder sandwiched between the major Great Himalayas to the south and the Kunlun mountain range to the north, is also home to a distinct and unique culture. With their unique customs and ways of life, the people of Ladakh are frequently praised for their humility and sense of realism.

The geographical impact on their groundedness

One of the most compelling reasons for the humble and grounded nature of the Ladakhi people is their geographic environment. Living in one of the most remote and challenging terrains in the world, they have developed a profound connection with nature. This deep bond with their surroundings fosters a sense of respect and humility that is evident in their daily lives. The harsh climatic conditions and the high altitude have necessitated a lifestyle that is both resilient and self-sufficient, qualities that are reflected in their interactions with others.

The role of limited exposure

Their comparatively little exposure to the outside world is another important feature that greatly contributes to their groundedness. Ladakh was cut off from most of the modern world until recently because of its harsh terrain and unfavourable political situation. Many of their traditional ways of life have survived because of their remoteness, which has also prevented the impact of rapid industrialization. Because of this, Ladakh's population has managed to hold onto a strong sense of cultural identity and communal values that are frequently lost in more urbanized environments.

Comparisons with Kashmiri people

As someone from Kashmir, I have observed that while the Kashmiri people are known for their sophistication and cultural richness, the people of Ladakh stand out for their unparalleled humility and kindness. This is not to undermine the grace and hospitality of the Kashmiri people but to highlight the striking contrast in demeanour. The simplicity and sincerity of the Ladakhis make them some of the most respectful and hospitable individuals one could meet.

The people of Ladakh are among the most kind and welcoming people you will ever meet because of their genuineness and simplicity.

Respecting other people

A fundamental aspect of Ladakhi culture is respect. The people of Ladakh have a great deal of respect for other people, whether they are interacting with residents or tourists. This respect creates an atmosphere of goodwill and appreciation for one another that cuts over age, socioeconomic class, and cultural divides. Their politeness is not merely a social custom; rather, it is an integral part of who they are.

As a medical officer in Ladakh, I have personally felt this regard. The general public also treats me with a great deal of respect, in addition to my colleagues at the office. I have not experienced this kind of respect in Kashmir, where a medical officer is frequently regarded as an ordinary worker. But in Ladakh, they genuinely regard you as an officer and value the assistance you give to the locals.

Unity as their funda

The core values of the Ladakhi way of life are community and solidarity. The people of Ladakh have formed a strong sense of togetherness since they live in an area where existence frequently depends on helping one another. They collaborate, enjoy life together, and help one another out when things become tough.

This solidarity is a cultural ethos that strengthens their ties to one another and cultivates a sense of community in addition to serving as a method of survival.

Conclusion

The people of Ladakh are a special blend of unity, humility, and respect that has been molded by their remote location and little exposure to outside influences. Their sense of community and groundedness teach us important lessons about human connection and simplicity. It is only to be hoped that these timeless ideals will flourish as modernization makes its way into the isolated valleys of Ladakh, protecting the region's rich cultural heritage.

As I bring this book to a close, I find myself reflecting on the journey that led to these pages. Echoes from Mountains and Valley is more than just a collection of my thoughts; it is a testament to the experiences, struggles, and hopes that have shaped me.

Through my writings, I have tried to capture the essence of life in the mountains and valleys—its beauty, its hardships, and the silent resilience of those who live within them. I have written about love and loss, about duty and sacrifice, about the quiet battles fought by teachers, doctors, and common people who often go unnoticed.

This book is not the end of my journey as a writer. It is just a milestone—a moment to pause, reflect, and acknowledge the people who have walked with me. The support of my family, the platform provided by The Kashmir Reader, and the presence of a special person in my life have been invaluable in shaping my thoughts and giving them a voice.

If these words resonate with even one reader, if they spark a thought, a reflection, or a deeper understanding of the world we live in, then this effort has been worthwhile. The echoes from these mountains and valleys will continue, and so will the stories yet to be told.

Thank you for being a part of this journey.